KV-374-500

If you're a teenager and someone tells you to slow down and be intentionally restful at times, you might roll your eyes...unless the 'why' behind the encouragement to rest was advice that could potentially save your life in the future. Consider this book crucial, life-saving advice. Bill Smith has written a biblical and genuinely helpful book that gives practical insight into joyfully living within your limitations.

Shelby Abbott
Campus minister; author, *Doubtless*

Bill's book is a boon to our harried students! At a time when the sabbath is a forgotten command (but never more needed!) and the digital places we go for rest only deplete us further, when our students are under greater demands than ever before and suffering the subsequent mental health fallout, *Rest* is a clarion call to heed the One who beckons the weary and heavy laden, promising to ease their burdens. Most importantly, although filled with practical application, this is not a book of rules! *Rest* urges our students to draw near to Jesus as the true source of refreshment, applying the healing balm of the gospel to harrassed sheep. I look forward to passing it on to the students in my congregation (including my children!).

David White
Pastor, Springton Lake PCA, Springton Lake,
Newtown Square, Pennsylvania;
author, *Sexual Sanity for Men*.

Dedication

To my friends, Paul Tripp and
Paul Keisling,
who regularly refresh me,
both physically and spiritually,
in more ways than I can count.

TRACK
DOCTRINE

REST

A STUDENT'S GUIDE TO

WILLIAM
P. SMITH

SERIES EDITED BY
JOHN PERRITT

CHRISTIAN
FOCUS

rym

Unless otherwise stated, Scripture quotations are from *The Holy Bible, English Standard Version*, copyright © 2001 by Crossway Bibles, a publishing ministry of Good News Publishers. Used by permission. All rights reserved. ESV Text Edition: 2011.

Scripture quotations marked NIV are taken from the Holy Bible, New International Version®, NIV® Copyright ©1973, 1978, 1984, 2011 by Biblica, Inc.® Used by permission. All rights reserved worldwide.

Copyright © William P. Smith 2024

paperback ISBN 978-1-5271-0844-8

ebook ISBN 978-1-5271-1148-6

10 9 8 7 6 5 4 3 2 1

First published in 2024
by
Christian Focus Publications Ltd,
Geanies House, Fearn,
Ross-shire, IV20 1TW, Great Britain
www.christianfocus.com

with

Reformed Youth Ministries,
1445 Rio Road East Suite 201D
Charlottesville, Virginia, 22911

Cover by MOOSE77

Printed and bound by Gutenberg, Malta

All rights reserved. No part of this publication may be reproduced, stored in a retrieval system, or transmitted, in any form, by any means, electronic, mechanical, photocopying, recording or otherwise without the prior permission of the publisher or a licence permitting restricted copying. In the U.K. such licences are issued by the Copyright Licensing Agency, 4 Battlebridge Lane, London, SE1 2HX www.cla.co.uk

CONTENTS

Series Introduction

Christianity is a religion of words, because our God is a God of words. He created through words, calls Himself the Living Word, and wrote a book (filled with words) to communicate to His children. In light of this, pastors and parents should take great efforts to train the next generation to be readers. *Track* is a series designed to do exactly that.

Written for students, the *Track* series addresses a host of topics in three primary areas: Doctrine, Culture, and the Christian Life. *Track's* booklets are theologically rich, yet accessible. They seek to engage and challenge the student without dumbing things down.

One definition of a track reads: *a way that has been formed by someone else's footsteps.* The goal of the *Track* series is to point us to that 'someone else'—Jesus Christ. The One who forged a track to guide His followers. While we cannot follow this track perfectly, by His grace and Spirit He calls us to strive to stay on the path. It is our prayer that this series of books would help guide Christ's Church until He returns.

In His service,

John Perritt
RYM's Director of Resources
Series Editor

Foreword

First, a confession. I started working on this book prior to the pandemic of Covid-19. That seems like such a long time ago. There have been many exhausting days, weeks and months since then, and if I'm honest, I probably have not recovered either physically or emotionally.

Which leads to a second confession, my embarrassment. I can only imagine the disbelieving looks from the people in my church when they hear I've written a book on rest—'You? What do you know about rest?'

That's a fair question. I've lived most of my adult life on the edge of trying to do more than I realistically can. But then again, so do many of the people in my church. Maybe that's true for you as well? Honestly, the only expert-rester I know is my cat … who's dedicated himself to making up for the rest of us.

But that brings me to my third conviction. I know that, without the things in this book that

I've practiced now for decades, I would be in a far, far worse place than I am.

Like you, I'm still a work in progress, but I've also experienced the goodness of what I've learned over the years. And I'm convinced that others can as well.

I'm reminded of the young man in his early twenties who teared up as he and I talked briefly about some of the things you're about to read. He hadn't learned them as a teen and was paying the price in his own life. I wish now that I'd learned and practiced them earlier as well.

This is some of my heart behind this little book. I hope you can learn from my mistakes. I hope you can start the process of resting sooner than I did. To that end, please know that I've stopped and prayed for you just now, that you take advantage as early as possible, of experiencing the glorious grace of our God as he leads you into the rest he has for you.

1. We Don't Rest Well

Americans are crazy busy.[1] Our world offers nearly unlimited opportunities and pairs them with impossible expectations. And we love it. We find the combination irresistible ... and yet, it's also crushing.

There's the never-ending list of things we could fill our time with—school, sports, work, music programs, drama clubs, chess clubs, clubs of all kinds, volunteer organizations, church youth groups—all good things that clamor for our attention and our participation.

And there's the list of people who think we can (and should!) do more than we already are—parents, grandparents, teachers, friends, teammates, coaches, shift-managers, pastors, youth-workers, boyfriends, girlfriends, church

---

1. I cannot improve on Kevin DeYoung's title for brevity or impact.

friends—all with some claim on our time, or at least, who think they have.

They want us to show up more often, to be more involved, to be more friendly, more outgoing, more welcoming, to produce more, to produce sooner and to produce better.

And because we know that we can always sleep a little less or rush through something a little more quickly, we pack more and more in, ending up busier than we were before.

We spin the gerbil-wheel faster and faster. We talk about not having any 'margin' in our lives, of how we're living under the 'tyranny of the urgent.' We feel tired. We look tired. And when people ask how we're doing, we tell them we are tired

And it never feels like there's any break, so we create breaks. We check out during the day by playing video games, watching videos, texting friends, scrolling through social media, posting to our own stories ... even our breaks are busy.

A busyness that's addictive. We find that we can't put our phones and devices down for long. Music and podcasts run constantly in the background. We binge-watch one show after another after another. We're always looking for the next thing to entertain us. Something that will keep us from having to think about all the things that everyone wants from us.

Only, we always seem to spend way more time being distracted than we planned for. And then we feel bad. Everything that we checked out from is still waiting for us, still needing to be done. And so, we can't shut down and end the day when we should.

We lose the boundary between work and rest and we end up oscillating back-and-forth between the two. We know how to work and we know how to be entertained. But we are not very good at resting. We're not good at quieting our souls in the middle of a frantic world that is in constant, exhausting motion, and so our 'resting' feels as frantic as the rest of life.

We don't know how to be refreshed at the deepest level of our being. The thought of sitting quietly, being still, alone with our thoughts and our God, feels unnatural. Unproductive. Unappealing. Like he's one more thing 'to do'; one more person with expectations we can't meet.

BUSYNESS, REST & IDOLATRY

That's the problem when good things—like living a full, engaged life—take over life; when they have no boundaries. A river running in its channel through a city gives life to the city. But when it overflows its banks so that all you can see is water, it's no longer a river. It's a flood. And now it's life-taking.

In the same way, when you try to get more life out of something than it was meant to give—when a good thing runs amuck—then it ends up damaging life.

This is what Scripture means when it talks about the danger of idolatry—of taking a good thing and making it an ultimate thing—of trying to find more life in some part of creation than in the One who created it (Rom. 1:25-32).

Idols—in this case, busyness as a way of life—never deliver on their promise to give you a good life. You believe that if you just cram a little bit more into your schedule—another activity; another distraction—then that will take away some of the pressure you're feeling and life will be good.

And yet, you discover that life isn't better. It's just busier. It's even less good now, than it was before.

Idols always leave you wanting more. They demand more and more time and energy from you, while they give you less and less return on each investment. And once you start down this road, it's impossible to stop.

Do you have an idea what some of those idols are for you—the things that never seem to satisfy you like you hoped they would?

What's the solution? Unsurprisingly, it's Jesus. Yes, you knew I was going to say that, right? But, it's still true.

He steps into this swirling, chaotic busyness that wears us down without filling us up and he says,

Come to me all who labor and are heavy laden, and I will give you rest. Take my yoke upon you, and learn from me for I am gentle and lowly in heart and you will find rest for your souls (Matt. 11:28-29).

Jesus promises deep, inner rest for those who live on treadmills and gerbil-wheels. He promises rest for those who are heavy laden. He offers a way of life that will help restore a work-life balance and navigate the expectations and opportunities that are not going to go away.

And Jesus offers that rest after having lived here, on this earth; after having experienced what it's like to be human.

He knows firsthand what it is to be a finite, human being who cannot possibly squeeze in all the demands and offers that people put in front of you.

He lived with those same expectations—from His mother, His brothers, His disciples, His friends, the religious leaders and the thousands of people who followed Him everywhere He went, all wanting something different from Him.

They offered Him countless opportunities—to serve, to heal, to teach, to grow His ministry and to do anything and everything they wanted Him to do. He lived under all the pressures that you and I do and, after having experienced all of that, He says, 'Come to me. There is a way of living here, in this chaotic world, where you can have rest and a light burden. Come to me for it. I know how to live it and I'll share that life with you.'

This book is an invitation to enter into that rest—to unplug and to enter into a world with Christ that ratchets down the crazy while He nourishes your soul.

MAIN POINT

Jesus offers rest to those who don't know how to stop.

QUESTIONS FOR REFLECTION

- Outside of school or your job, what do you spend most of your time doing?
- What stresses you out the most?
- Do you really believe Jesus can help you with rest? Be honest.

2. A God Who Rests

If someone walked up to you and asked, 'Who is God?' How would you answer that? There're a lot of good answers … as well as some pretty bad ones.

One of the very first things that God tells us about Himself is that He likes to work (Gen. 1)—that He likes the process of taking something chaotic and useless and making it beautiful and productive. He tells us that there is value and dignity to work because God Himself, is a Worker.

And we learn that God enjoys what He produces—that as He steps back from what He's made, he says, 'It's good.' Can you see Him smile when something is finally what He always knew it could be?

There's a steady rhythm of His enjoyment throughout the chapter as He makes something, declares, 'It's good' … then later after He makes something else, says that, 'It's good.' On and on—it's good, it's good, it's good—until He gets to the very end of what He is creating, and he says, verse 31, 'It's very good' (see Gen. 1:10, 12 18, 21, 25).

But then He does something that He hasn't done before. He stops working. And He rests (Gen. 2:2). And you learn that as important as work is to God and as central as it is to His character; work is not His primary identity.

He doesn't lose Himself in His work. He's not a slave to some inner, out-of-control compulsion. He's not trying to make up for some underlying insecurity in Himself. Instead, His making flows from His being—from who He is.

And so does His resting. They are two different ways that God expresses Himself in this physical world—two different, but equally important ways. They're not antagonistic impulses inside of Him that He ping-pongs back-and-forth between.

Rather, He engages His world and enjoys it by producing and by creating—by working—and he engages His world and enjoys it, by resting.

WHY DID GOD REST?

Now, why does He rest? Because He's tired? Worn out and needs a break? No. He tells us that He rests because He was all done (Gen. 2:2). Everything was now the way He wanted it. And that tells us something about rest.

As we'll see in Chapter 6 of this book, rest is not the same as inactivity. God is still active in His resting as He keeps the world running. But He's no longer creating and so He rested from adding value to what He already made.

Rest then, is not the mere absence of work, nor is resting the same as endless relaxation. That means that how God rests might be a different kind of rest than you are used to thinking about.

When we take something good from God's creation and make too much of it, we paradoxically don't have more of it. We have less, because we no longer understand it like God does. Take the case of work and rest.

Some of us idolize work. We elevate it to a place in our lives where it controls us and we become workaholics—people who are never able to stop as we try to justify our existence by how much we do and on how well we do it.

Others of us, however, idolize rest. We become hedonists. We lose ourselves in pleasure and entertainment, believing that heaven is a never-ending vacation.

But neither of those distortions are how God works or rests. They're caricatures of what He does. And so, if we're going to escape the busyness of this world, then we need to understand what rest means to Him. Or, to say it slightly differently, we need to see what His resting tells us about Him.

THREE THINGS REST TELLS US ABOUT GOD

First, it tells us that he has complete and total control over all that He has made. You can't rest if you're afraid that someone will come along and undo what you've done.

Do you know what that's like? Like when you're working on a group project for school and you're sharing a remote document. You can pour tons of time into it and get it to where you're finally happy with it … but you can't rest. Why?

Because as soon as you click out, you keep wondering, 'What are they doing? Are they changing things?' And so, you keep going back to check and see what the rest of your group has done and whether you like it or not. You can't rest. Why? Because what you did—what you evaluated as 'good'—can be undone. And when that happens, you might not think it's as good.

God doesn't have that problem. He doesn't have to be constantly vigilant. He can rest without worrying if someone's going to undo what He's done. What He has made is not ever at risk of ending up differently than what He ultimately wants it to be. Because He is all powerful over His creation, He can rest.

Second, God can rest because He completes what He sets out to do with His unmatched power.

He doesn't finish creation, sit down and go, 'Shoot! I just remembered something else that I wanted to do. Ugh. Now I have to get up and go fix that.' He's not forgetful and He doesn't keep churning inside with new ideas.

Have you ever woken up in the middle of the night and thought, 'Man, I wish I'd thought of this before. It would have been so easy to incorporate it earlier. I wonder if I should go back and add it in? If I do, that's going to take a lot of time … but I don't know … maybe it'd be worth it?'

God doesn't have those kinds of thoughts. He knows what He wants for His world when He creates it and He keeps working at it until He's done.

And because He's done, He can rest. No more tinkering. No more adjusting. It's good. So good, that it's very good. So very good, that He rests.

Third, God rests to take pleasure in what He does. It's only after He evaluates the total package of what He made—after He takes in everything that He's finished by His power—that He rests. It's a shift from enjoying Creation for what He can do with it to enjoying Creation for what it is.

His enjoyment goes from a verb to a noun. Hang with me. This isn't going to be a boring grammar lesson, for those of you who don't like grammar.

God's rest is no longer based in activity—in a verb: in creating. But now His enjoyment is in a distinct reality—in a noun: in Creation itself as it perfectly, reflects visibly how amazing He is (Rom. 1:20, Ps. 19:1-4).

And He rests from building a place where creatures can live so that He can be with His creatures—especially with human beings who reflect Him better than anything else in the universe (Gen. 1:27, 3:8). He rests to share His world with His children.

He doesn't lose Himself in His creation or try to escape it by running from it. He enjoys it and He enjoys relationships within it. That's an important part of what it means to rest.

MAIN POINT

God teaches us to honor our work and rest.

QUESTIONS FOR REFLECTION

- Do you attach your identity to your work?
- How are you tempted to overwork or over-rest?
- Do you take pleasure in the work to which God calls you?

3. God's People Rest

Let me say something really obvious – sin is bad. We all know it has brought endless misery into our lives, but have you thought about its impact on rest? How it distorts rest?

Genesis 1 introduces you to God, the Worker—a God who likes to work and who likes what He produces. Genesis 2 shows us that He enjoys resting as much as He does working.

Then as you keep reading, you're introduced to human beings; creatures whom God makes in His image (Gen. 1:26-27). And God takes these beings who are like Him, puts them in a Garden and tells them to work it and take care of it (Gen. 2:15).

Do you see the symmetry? God is the capital-W, Worker and his images are lower-case-w, workers. What then follows logically? Here's God, the Worker-and-Rester, and so you expect His images to reflect Him by being workers-and-resters ... only, they're not.

Sin enters the picture. Humans break their friendship with God and become distorted pictures of Him. They no longer work or rest like He does—they become rest-less.

God refuses to accept that new state of affairs, however, and so He set in motion plans to repair Creation by sending His Son to renew it. An early part of that plan involved building a friendship with a man named Abraham.

That friendship would extend to Abraham's descendants, but God knew they would have no idea how to be friends with him. Do you struggle knowing how to be friends with God? One way He taught us to be friends with Him is by giving us commands that reflect His own character and nature.

One of those commands is about something called the Sabbath day—a full day in every week, to rest. Now this is a command that God thinks is just great. And there's something that makes the Sabbath command unique. Something that makes it different from the others.

While most of the other laws start with something you are not to do—you shall have no other gods before me; you shall not make an image of me for yourself; you shall not misuse my name; you shall not murder, steal, lie, covet, etc.—this one starts with something you shall do: you shall remember the Sabbath day, to keep it holy.

God is telling you that the nature of this day is fundamentally positive. It's not a day that is first and foremost defined by restriction—by things you do not do—instead, it starts with something that you do. You remember. You keep.

As you make your way through Scripture, you discover that this command is really special to God. He references Sabbath and keeping Sabbath more often than he does any of the other commands in the five books that Moses wrote. There is something really special about the Sabbath.

It's so special that God later speaks of it as a day of delight, one that leads to joy (Isa. 58:13-14). It's a day of happiness. One that doesn't merely sustain life, but that gives life—that lets you enter the coming week personally restored with your priorities reoriented around God and His desires.

THE FORGOTTEN COMMANDMENT

The fourth commandment is something though that has caused a lot of confusion. It's a command that many Christians today attach negative thoughts to. It's one that many people see as optional. Or even see as burdensome. A command that infringes on our freedom to do what we want, when we want.

And so, I've been in a number of conversations where someone asks, 'But why? Why should we Sabbath a whole day?' Maybe you're thinking something like that now.

If you are, have you ever wondered, 'If I'm not going to obey one of the Ten Commandments, isn't the burden of proof more on me to give a reason for why I don't, instead of asking why I should?'

And, having been in these conversations, I could imagine someone saying, 'Well, Jesus said that He came to fulfill the law, so this one is no longer binding on us.'

And there is something to that, but there's also a lot of confusion that gets mixed into that response as well.

For instance, no one argues that Jesus fulfilling the law means that the rest of the Ten Commandments can all be scrapped. That we can now dishonor our parents because Jesus fulfilled the law. Or that it's okay to murder, steal what we like, lie when we can get away with it and covet what someone else has.

None of those commands are erased when Jesus said that He came to fulfill the law, so, why should the fourth commandment, which is in that same list?

Here's where it's helpful to understand that God's law operates on three different levels:

- there is a moral component to God's law that is binding on all people for all time, and
- there's a ceremonial aspect to His law that pointed forward to the Messiah and to what He would accomplish,
- and there's a civil component that was for the purpose of governing the nation of Israel when it was uniquely organized as a theocracy (i.e., when the nation was led by priests and kings who got their authority from God).

Those three levels were all in play under the Old Covenant, but not in the New.

God used the civil laws to fashion a people for Himself from whom the Messiah would come, while the ceremonial laws prepared them for what the Messiah would do when He came.

After Christ lived, died and rose again, the ceremonial and civil laws could then be set aside since their purpose is now fulfilled. And so there are aspects of the Sabbath in the Mosaic law that are no longer in force—for instance, we no longer stone people for breaking the Sabbath (Exod. 35:2, Num. 15:32-36).

But the Sabbath is more than a ceremonial or civil law. As one of the Ten Commandments, it's in a different category—the moral category which reflects God's eternal nature and His character.

Check out the New Testament passages sometime that might make you wonder if Sabbath is still important (Rom. 14:1-6, Gal. 4:10, Col. 2:16-23). What will you find there? The context surrounding each one involves people who think that what they do— their obedience to certain human rules and constraints—somehow makes them better in God's eyes.

Observing the Sabbath, however, is not a means of making God happy with you— that's what Jesus accomplished through His sacrificial death and resurrection. But keeping the Sabbath is also not a temporal command that is superseded.

You can see its enduring nature simply because it's listed as one of the Ten or by looking closely at the rationale behind the command in Exodus 20 where God says:

> *Remember the Sabbath day, to keep it holy. ... For in six days the LORD made heaven and earth, the sea, and all that is in them, and rested on the seventh day. Therefore, the LORD blessed the Sabbath day and made it holy* (vv. 8,11).

What reason does God give for resting one day out of seven? There are two, neither of which are based on any human needs within ancient Israelite society:

- First, it's something God Himself did— He rested on the seventh day.
- Second, it's something He built into the Creation.

Before sin ever entered the picture, God blessed one day. He made it special. Holy. In a perfect, sinless world, God took one day and sanctified it.

That means when you keep the Sabbath, you're not making one day special. You're simply entering into the specialness of that one day that already exists. Your obedience does not create a holy day. You're simply keeping the day what it already is—holy.

And by doing so, you're aligning yourself with the nature of the universe instead of running against the grain of what God has established for you and for His world.

I know this is a lot to take in. If you're like many Christians today, the idea of a Sabbath day is pretty foreign. But, hang in there. As you'll see, the Sabbath command is a gift. And if you're stressed right now from being hyper-busy, ask yourself, 'Is it possible that that might be related to not having this day in my life?'

MAIN POINT

The Sabbath command offers blessing to God's people.

QUESTIONS FOR REFLECTION

- Do you have any negative thoughts about the Sabbath command? If so, what are they?
- Have you ever tried to practice the Sabbath?
- What's holding you back from trying to take one day to rest? Does that idea scare you?

4. What Goes into Resting

Why do you think people hate Jesus today? If you asked an unbeliever what bothers them most about Jesus, what might be at the top of the list?

It's weird to realize that 'rest' was one of the most controversial issues that Jesus faced during His earthly lifetime. Now, why is that?

Back then, people had added so many rules and restrictions about what you could and couldn't do on the Sabbath that they thought Jesus was regularly doing something He shouldn't … and they felt very free to let Him know it (Matt. 12:1-8, Luke 6:6-11, 13:10-17).

Part of the reason they added so many rules is that God is relatively silent about how you go about remembering and keeping the Sabbath day holy. That tells you there is a lot of freedom in this command.

God affirms that freedom in the New Testament by telling you not to judge someone for how they do or don't observe a Sabbath day (Rom. 14:5-6, Col. 2:16-23). Now that Christ has fulfilled the law, we have even greater freedom than the Israelites did in how we Sabbath.

Even for the Israelites, however, there were very few principles they had to keep in mind. We can boil them down to two attitudes that we'll look at in this chapter and two actions that we'll unpack in the next. The attitudes reorient us away from trust in ourselves to trust in our God.

TWO ATTITUDES

First, we rest because we trust Him to provide for what we need even if we are not working that day to produce something for ourselves.

God spells out that kind of trust explicitly when He fed His people with manna in the wilderness—with bread that appeared in the morning on the desert floor that they gathered six days out of seven (Exod. 16:4-5).

On most days He told them to pick up as much as they needed for just that one day, but on the sixth day they were to gather twice as much because there wouldn't be any on the seventh (Exod. 16:21-23).

God made that exception so that His people could rest one day from working. But in order to do that, they had to trust that He would give them enough on the sixth day and that it wouldn't spoil overnight like it did on other days (Exod. 16:24-26).

He was helping them learn that He loved them and would take care of them when they obeyed Him, even when His commands didn't line up with how they were used to thinking.

Have you ever participated in a 'trust fall'? You close your eyes and fall backwards, as a group of friends catch you. It's kind of scary, because your eyes are closed and there's a chance your friends might drop you.

Obviously, God is not like that. You can close your eyes and trust Him to take care of you … but that doesn't mean you can trust Him to give you everything you want. Trusting Him by resting when He says to rest will honor Him and be good for you, but it will not give you everything that you're used to having.

There are implications—costs—if you choose not to work seven shifts a week, study every night or train every day. You may not make the same amount of money as other people do. You will have to adjust your study schedule to get your homework done, which may cut into other activities you want to do. You might not have the same conditioning as other athletes or musicians.

Obeying the Lord may not get you what you want because obeying Him is not a means to an end. So be careful how you think about obedience. It's not a strategy—it's not a way of putting God in your debt so that He feels obligated to come through for you.

Rather, obeying the Lord is how we keep our hearts and lives in step with His as we trust Him to give us what we need (which is not always the same as what we want)

The second attitude is related to the first, and that is we rest because we trust God to run the world without needing our help.

God watches over His people and so we don't have to be constantly vigilant, constantly active, to make sure that everything in our life turns out well (Ps. 121:1-8).

The reason He can care for us individually is because nothing in the universe is outside His control (Matt. 28:18). He actively rules over everything in creation, bringing it to a conclusion that will realize all His hopes and longings of being with His people forever, in a world unmarred by sin (Rev. 21:8).

That's your destiny as a child of God. A destiny that nothing will keep you from. You don't have to strive and work endlessly to give yourself a good life because Jesus has already secured one for you.

And you don't have to fear what might happen if you're not hard at work or always watching your back, since you can trust that the Lord will take whatever does or does not happen to you and use it for your good (Rom. 8:28).

Do you think of yourself as a controlling person? Some of you probably struggle with this more than others, but this second attitude exposes that tendency in most of us. It's often harder for us to let go of things than we realize. We don't want to entrust them to God.

So once a week, to help our hearts grasp this reality, we let go of the steering wheel of our lives. We rest—actively reminding ourselves that what happens to us does not depend solely on the sum total of what we do or decide.

Resting expresses our confidence that God is the one who runs this world and everything in it. And because He does, there is absolutely no danger of anything spinning out of control or ending up in a place that will eternally frustrate Him.

And since it won't frustrate Him for eternity, then it won't upset us either. I hope that reality starts to let your heart rest a little bit better today.

MAIN POINT

God faithfully provides for His creation, so we can rest by trusting in His goodness.

QUESTIONS FOR REFLECTION

- How do you seek to control your life?
- What do you struggle to entrust to God?
- What are some specific things God has provided for you today?

5. What (else) Goes into Resting?

Have you ever streamed a show that starts with a recap of previous episodes to refresh what you've seen? Sometimes we choose to skip the recap, but let me refresh our minds real quick. What have we covered so far?

- Jesus offers rest for busy people.
- God honors both work and rest.
- God's Sabbath offers blessing to His people.
- Our rest is connected to trusting God's goodness and control.

Resting also expresses our trust that God will provide for us and that He is able to run the world well without our constant help, but what does it involve?

Again, the Sabbath command gives very few particulars, but two worth noting are:

1) that it has something to do with worship, and 2) something to do with not working.

WORSHIP

Let's take worship first. Exodus 20:10 tells us that this day is a Sabbath *to the Lord your God*. In other words, it's not simply a day off. It's not a day where you kick back and reinforce that life is all about you and about relaxing. It's not a day where you indulge yourself and become the center of your world.

Instead, it's a day that has a special focus on the Lord. Yes, in one sense, all of life is worship. All of life is oriented around God and lived consciously before the face of God so that there is no sacred-secular division of your life. Your work—your career, your studies, your chores at home—as well as your rest, are part of worship.

And yet, there is something special about the Sabbath so that it has an intentional 'to the Lord-ness' about it. He is the end that you direct yourself toward on this day.

And so, principle one, the purpose of the day has something to do with furthering your worship of God because it is set-apart *to the Lord*.

REST

Second, it's rest-filled. God rested on the seventh day; now you rest on the seventh day. But what does 'rest' mean? Exodus 20:9 says:

Six days you shall labor and do all your work, but the seventh day is a Sabbath to the Lord your God. On it you shall not do any work.

What is this work you are not to do? Very simply, it's the work that you did the other six days when you labored like God did. It's the work of creating and making things to enjoy or that might benefit others. It's the work of providing for present needs and future desires, both for yourself and for the people you love.

You take all that good work that you've been doing all week and you take a break from it. Yes, you still engage in life-sustaining activities. You still get food for yourself. You still help your parents out with a younger sibling. You still take the dog for a walk.

But you cease from the regular, optional kind of work that you were doing the rest of the week so that this day has a certain 'not six-ness' to it. And instead, you enter in and enjoy what God has created and what He has provided for you.

And this is not just for you or for a couple special people. Instead,

On [the Sabbath] you shall not do any work, neither you, nor your son or daughter, nor your male or female servant, nor your animals, nor any foreigner residing in your towns (Exod. 20:10 NIV).

God's command creates a new social order so that who works and who rests is not divided along gender lines, class lines or ethnic lines. Instead, the entire community of God's people enters into a rhythm of work and rest. Everyone gets to provide for their own needs from their own labor *and* everyone gets to take a break from providing for themselves.

And you don't get to take a break because you've been productive enough earlier. It's not because you've earned it. You rest, simply because you have joined yourself to the people of God and have come under the protection of the God who Works and Rests.

Those are the two principles in this passage. Keeping the Sabbath day has an intentional God-ward direction to it and something to do with ceasing from the self-providing labor of the other six days.

So, when you think about the Sabbath and about what you're going to do or not do, it's helpful to ask yourself two questions: 'Will this thing that I'm thinking about doing … will it help me worship *and* will it help me rest?'

If the answer to either one is 'No' then it's probably not a good Sabbath activity and you'd be better off saving it for another day.

But if the answer to both is 'Yes' then this is what the day was made for. Go ahead then and do your worship-rest thing while you call the Sabbath a delight.

And as you enjoy the day and as you rest, let it remind you that there is a sense in which Jesus also rests. That right now He's seated at the right hand of God—seated, not laboring. Why?

Because on the cross He said, 'It is finished' (John 19:28-30), meaning, 'It's all done. All my work on behalf of my people is complete. I have provided everything that they need to live with me forever. There's nothing more to do.'

That's why Hebrews, Chapter 10 tells us:

And every priest stands daily at his service, offering repeatedly the same sacrifices, which can never take away sins [they never rest, because they can't]. But when Christ had offered for all time a single sacrifice for sins, he sat down at the right hand of God, waiting from that time until his enemies should be made a footstool for his feet. For by a single offering he has perfected for all time those who are being sanctified (Heb. 10:11-14).

His single offering was enough to perfect you, to take away your sins so that you are in this moment, being sanctified—so that you are set apart, made holy—so that you will fit perfectly into the sanctified time and space that Jesus sovereignly rules over.

He is resting right now because He finished His work of providing what you need to restore your relationship with Him and to restore your relationship with work and with rest.

Because He rests, you also can rest. You can cease laboring to make a life for yourself and you can gratefully, joyfully, embrace the life He has given you.

Take Sabbath seriously. Rest. Worship. Enjoy. And let this little weekly reminder whet your appetite for an eternity of life with this One who worked so hard for you, so that you could rest with Him.

MAIN POINT

*Resting involves an element of worshipping the
Lord and taking a break from providing
for yourself.*

QUESTIONS FOR REFLECTION

- What gets you more excited about Sunday: getting up later or being able to worship with God's people?
- What are the main ways you work now (i.e., studying, practices, part-time job, etc.)? How challenging would it be to rest from those?
- Your attitude toward rest shows who you trust to give you a better future—either yourself and your work, or Jesus and His. What does your attitude tell you about who you trust more?

6. Resting is not Mere Inactivity

Have you ever encountered anyone sleep walking? It's strange because they really are asleep but they're also using their body to walk around. How can they be resting and active at the same time? While that answer would take us too far off topic, sleep walking shows us something helpful about our rest. There are times when resting can involve activity.

The Sabbath is God's mercy to us to help slow us down, to reorient our lives around trusting Him, and to enter into His enjoyment of the world that He's made.

It's a day for looking outward, not inward—outward to God, but also outward to images of God. And so, as you study a passage like Matthew 12:1-14, you discover there are two conditions under the Sabbath when it's not only right, but necessary to be active—times when you should get up and do something on this weekly rest day.

In the first section, verses 1-8, Jesus' disciples are picking grain on the Sabbath as they pass through a field. And there are Pharisees there, watching them. Evaluating them and openly criticizing what they're doing, claiming that it's not lawful for them to do so. Shaming and embarrassing them in front of Jesus, their rabbi who's responsible for their behavior.

Now, be careful. They're not saying, 'Your disciples are breaking God's law.' Their critiques come from a long list of highly detailed regulations that the rabbinic authorities added to Scripture. Regulations that were then elevated to the same level as what God said. To put it bluntly, these regulations weren't in the Bible.

Jesus responds to them with a story from King David's life when he and his men ate bread that only the priests were allowed to eat, as defined by the law of Moses (see 1 Sam. 21:1-6).

They did what wasn't lawful by human standards, but far from rebuking them, God preserved a record of it in Scripture, effectively arguing that their need outweighed the Mosaic prohibition.

Meeting human needs takes precedence in God's mind over conforming to any external code of good behavior. His heart is that both David's men and the disciples should do whatever is necessary to meet their physical need.

That's the first condition for being active on the Sabbath. Here's the second. Jesus goes from there to a synagogue and encounters a man with a withered hand (Matt. 12:9-14). Predictably, the Pharisees challenge Him about healing on the Sabbath, suggesting that He should wait for another day.

Jesus replies that if they saw one of their animals struggling—like maybe one of their sheep fell into a pit—wouldn't they pull it out? Obviously, they would and Jesus points out that human beings are worth far more than any animal and so He heals the man.

These then are the two conditions under which you act on the Sabbath, even if it looks like you're working—either to meet a need or to relieve suffering.

You don't create situations where you have to work, but Jesus is effectively saying, 'If you see someone struggling, don't make them put up with that for another day. In fact, don't wait one more moment! Do what you can do now.' And so, he concludes, Matthew 12:12, that it is lawful to do good on the Sabbath.

Do you see how different that is from the Pharisees and their worldview? They're all about restricting activity. It's not enough for them to hear God say they're not to work one day a week. Instead, they have to define exactly what work is and what it's not.

And then they have to make sure that they and everyone else follow their laws so that no one can accuse them of doing anything wrong. Their agenda is to protect themselves by establishing how good they are.

Now, was there any way that they could have known that their approach was wrong— that they were badly out of step with God? Well, look at what comes out of their lives:

- They're critical of others.
- They try to shame people who disagree with them.
- They'd rather have other people suffer— being hungry or physically impaired— to pay for their way of life.

- And they start planning to kill this one who wants to create a wonderful world to live in (Matt. 12:14).

Nothing good comes out of their approach. And Jesus is nothing like them. He is the Lord of the Sabbath (Matt. 12:8) who desires mercy, not sacrifice (Matt. 12:7)—not yours or anyone else's—in order to create a beautiful world. One in which a Sabbath rest is restful for you and where you have been released to love people, by helping provide rest for others as well.

And the best part? Jesus offers himself to make that world possible. It's no accident that immediately before this passage Jesus said:

Come to me, all who labor and are heavy laden, and I will give you rest. Take my yoke upon you, and learn from me, for I am gentle and lowly in heart, and you will find rest for your souls. For my yoke is easy, and my burden is light (Matt. 11:28-30).

Why could He say that? Because He would do the work of earning God's approval by obeying God in everything. And if you're yoked to Jesus, then the goodness that He earned, counts for you so that what's His, becomes yours.

And because He's yoked to you, what's yours becomes His. He takes your sins—your failures to think of others and to be merciful to them—and He makes those failures His own. And because they're His, He ended up being shamed for them.

The Father forsook Him—abandoned Him on the cross because the shame of what you and I have done was too much to bring into the throne room of God.

Jesus endured that shame in our place. Experienced God being disappointed with him so that God will never turn away from you. He yoked you to Himself so that you will never be embarrassed in God's presence.

That's the radical kind of mercy that God loves. And that's a God who's worth coming to—one who will give you rest for your soul so that you're set free to be merciful to others, blessing them—actively—like He's been merciful to you.

MAIN POINT

It's good to act on the Sabbath to meet some-one's need or to relieve suffering.

QUESTIONS FOR REFLECTION

- Can you remember a time when you saw someone in need and helped them, when you really just wanted to rest?
- The Pharisees were more concerned with their idea of goodness, rather than with actually being good. Do you see that tendency in your own heart (like I do in mine)?
- Do you regularly meditate on and pray about Jesus' mercy to you? That will soften your heart so that you'll want to be merciful to others even when it's inconvenient for you.

7. Elements of Rest

━━━━━━

Have you ever been exhausted? I don't just mean really tired. I mean so physically and mentally worn out that you can't imagine going on? In 1 Kings 19, we find Elijah utterly exhausted and totally demoralized. He's unrested and asking God to take his life (v. 4). What happened?

Just one day earlier, he squared off against 450 false prophets of Baal who were leading Israel away from the Lord (1 Kings 18:16-45). Elijah challenged them to a contest that would prove who the real God was—their Baal or Israel's YHWH, who had loved and rescued His people.

And YHWH came through, sending fire from heaven to consume the sacrifice that Elijah prepared, demonstrating that He alone is the one true God. Israel recognized the truth of His reality and killed the false prophets. God then blessed them by ending a devastating three-year drought. This is the high-water mark of Elijah's ministry.

The very next day, however, Queen Jezebel threatened to kill him and he ran for his life (1 Kings 19:1-3). Now, why? What's wrong with him?

The way you answer that question will determine what you think he needs in order to be restored. Is he experiencing an emotional breakdown? Physically worn out? Sinning against God?

Your answer in each case will lead you to a different intervention. And here's where you need to be careful, because the modern age tempts you to reduce Elijah down to one dimension and then focus on that dimension as the root cause of his running. If you do that, then you will focus on it as the primary issue that needs to be remediated.

God is not that reductionistic. What does he do? He feeds Elijah, twice (1 Kings 19:5-6, 8). Lets him sleep (v.6). Validates his experience (v. 7). Draws him out (v. 9), stages an intervention (vv. 11-13) and instructs him, reorienting him to what is true about the world and to the additional resources he has in it (vv.15-18).

In short, God takes a multi-dimensional approach to Elijah because Elijah is a multi-dimensional being.

In order to rest well, you also have to take into account the various parts of who you are. Let's consider three:

1. You are a unity of a *spirit* ...
2. in a *body* ...
3. that God has placed in a *community*.

Resting well should address at least those three aspects. Here are a few thoughts of what that would mean for a weekly rest day.

Spiritual rest includes time to intentionally connect with God through praise, prayer, Scripture and instruction. While these elements should take place in the public worship service, don't overlook making time for them privately as well. You might find it helpful to have a theological-devotional book that you're working through because you want to study a particular topic or because the author 'speaks' to you and to how you experience life.

I also set aside a longer time once a week for quiet thinking and reflection. I allow the Lord to bring things to my mind that I'll quickly scribble down on a notepad or take time to think through from different angles. These are often thoughts I've had earlier in the week that I need to consider a little longer, but ones that got pushed out by the busyness of life.

If you're not used to this kind of meditating, you might want to start with fifteen minutes and go from there. I find that time extremely helpful for bringing my mind and emotions out of the churning place they can live in during the rest of the week.

Physical rest can certainly include a nap, but should also involve things that let you enjoy God's good creation—eat good food, go on a hike or ride your bike, visit a park, spend the afternoon at the beach, play a game with your friends, throw or kick a ball around, grab a frisbee, etc.

And don't forget your nature as a *communal* being. Take time to rest with your friends and family. Sharing a meal or doing something together reminds you that your identity as a person does not depend on productivity—on what you do for others or on what they do for you.

Resting in community grounds your security in mutual love—on being embedded in a web of relationships—which lets you further unwind mentally and emotionally.

MISCELLANEOUS QUESTIONS

1. *Now, does it matter which day you rest?* Under the Old Covenant, the community rested on the last day of the week—on Saturday. Clearly, after Christ rose, the New Testament believers talk about 'the Lord's' Day' as special (Rev. 1:10)—our Sunday.

    In general, it would be better to rest along with the majority of God's people, but some people can't because of their work schedule (Matt. 12:5). For them, what's important is not the day, but the work-six-rest-one rhythm.

2. *What about activities that you don't ordinarily do during the week?* For instance, can cutting the grass be restful if you're inside studying all week? How about going for a run? Baking something in the kitchen?

    Here, the important consideration is not the activity, but the effect that the activity has on you.

    If cutting the grass becomes something that drives you to get it finished, if running morphs into being upset if you don't hit a certain time, or if your culinary creation leaves you frazzled with a roomful of dirty dishes, then those don't sound like good rest activities.

On the other hand, if what you're doing remains in that light, fun space that doesn't cause angst or frustration, then enjoy!

3. *How about activities that you turn to for entertainment during the week—like reading a novel, watching videos or playing an online game?*

The same principle in question 2 applies here as well. If the things you're considering become a compulsive activity that you can't stop, then by definition, that's not rest. If they fill your heart and mind in ways that don't fill the Creator's, that's also not rest.

But if they leave you refreshed and you can put them down without being absorbed by them, then maybe they can be a healthy part of resting.

Remember, God doesn't give a strict list of do's and don'ts. Learning what is and is not restful takes time and experience— what works well for you may not be what serves someone else.

Here again, there's room to grow. God gives us principles along with a huge world in which to practice them. He then removes the fear of failure by redeeming us. So, take His freedom seriously. Try things and ask yourself what leaves you refreshed and doesn't consume you as you learn a healthier way to rest.

MAIN POINT

Resting should be multi-dimensional so that it includes at least physical, spiritual and communal components.

QUESTIONS FOR REFLECTION

- What else could you try doing that would feed you spiritually, apart from going to church?
- What kinds of physical activities could you do to rest that would leave you refreshed, not worn out or feeling pressured?
- Who would you like to connect with relationally this next Lord's Day? What might you suggest doing with them?

8. Rhythms of Rest

———

Imagine if you woke up every morning, ate an entire bag of candy and then washed it down with a couple energy drinks. (If that describes your morning routine now, please stop).

Starting your morning like that would negatively affect the rest of your day. Your stomach would feel terrible, you'd probably get a headache and you'd have other long-term issues as well.

Conversely, a healthy diet has a positive impact and gives you a chance at a much higher quality of life. That's similar to what the Sabbath does in setting the stage for the rest of the week.

It resets how we approach all of life by reminding us that our working is entirely contingent on God working. It helps us recall that the only reason we can work is because he works, giving us the energy, resources, abilities and opportunities that we need, in order to work.

And so, this weekly rest-day invites us to repent of forgetting the foundation for why we can work while it renews our focus as we enter into a new week of work.

But does that mean we have to wait for this one day in order to be renewed and reset? Think again about Genesis 1 and you realize, 'No. There are daily rest-reminders that we can and should build into our weeks as well.'

At the end of each day in Genesis 1, God doesn't fully end his act of creating, but he does pause it for that day. Each day, after He's accomplished what He set out to do, He stops, steps back and analyzes what he's done. He sees that what He did was good and He communicates that assessment to us (Gen. 1:4, 10, 12, 18, 21, 25).

In other words, He mini-Sabbaths. Each day He does things that share the same form and content of the one day He makes holy. He does things daily that anticipate *the* Sabbath. He builds in mini-patterns—daily patterns—of work and pausing from work.

And you hear an echo of Him sharing this regular pause at the end of the day with Adam and Eve before sin broke their fellowship. They were used to God coming to meet them in the cool of the evening (Gen. 3:8). What was that time?

It was an opportunity to reconnect with Him—to feel the goodness of Him at the close of another work day, in His very good world. It was a mini-Sabbath.

Now that sin has entered the picture, those mini-rest times with Him are all the more vital. And so, you see Jesus often withdrawing to lonely places to pray (Luke 5:16; see also Matt. 14:23, Mark 1:35, Luke 9:18, 9:28) or when He needed to make weighty decisions (Matt. 26:36-46, Luke 6:12-16).

If the Son of God didn't think He could live without intentionally and regularly setting aside this kind of time throughout the week, then you and I can't either. We need daily rest, not just weekly, to:

- cease from work,
- reflect on the past day,
- enjoy God's creation,
- connect with God,
- connect with people,
- quiet our hearts and minds in a chaotic world,

- and get ready to re-enter the world the next day.

While the weekly rest-day can teach you what work and rest are like, you have to practice it daily for it to influence your attitudes and decisions throughout the whole week.

Let me try to give you a picture of what I mean. Think of the Sabbath day as a *sine wave* with a frequency of one week, so that one wavelength spans seven days.

If you shorten the wavelength to a single day, you increase the frequency of rest throughout the week. That rest is smaller—shorter and not as intense—but it's more regular. And it keeps the same basic shape as the longer wavelength so that there's a regular rhythm of rest that now impacts the whole week.

But if you can shorten the wavelength, couldn't you also lengthen it? What would happen if you stretched it out to, say, three months or even a year?

That's what people think of as a personal retreat—a time when you pull back from the regular routines of life for a day or a weekend in order to experience a kind of restoration that ordinarily there's no time for.

It's an opportunity to think about where your life has been and where you're going. A time when you reflect more broadly on your life, as you include all the elements of a weekly Sabbath. A time when you ask things like:

- How have I grown and matured since the last time I asked this question?
- What is the Lord doing in my life right now and how do I work with him?
- What opportunities and/or challenges am I likely to face in the next few months?

I would imagine that some of you reading this have gone on a youth retreat before. The entire design behind a retreat is to 'retreat'—to pull back—from our typical way of living and enter into a weekend or week that has a different rhythm and routine.

Along those lines, a personal retreat is a time where you hit 'pause' in order to be more deeply restored and renewed. And it's a time that won't seem odd, because you're simply extending the kinds of things you've already been practicing both daily and weekly.

Depending on where you are in life, you may not be able to have a personal retreat like the one I'm describing. If you're a teenager, this would be hard to do. However, you could seek to retreat from some of the busyness in your life. Here are some potential ideas:

- For a week, try to have an earlier bedtime.
- Instead of looking at your phone at bedtime, try reading a book.
- Wake up without your phone for the first hour of your day.
- In the morning, take some time to pray, read the Word and meditate.
- Make some time to be in God's creation 2-3 times a week.
- Try to decrease your screen-time from whatever your current average is.
- Say 'no' to some extracurriculars and clubs you're involved in.
- Take fifteen minutes to think of a few ways you could serve people in your home, neighborhood or church.

All of these are some ideas that can actually help you rest. Do you hear how different mini-Sabbaths and personal retreats are from what our world usually offers as ways to unplug? Some of these are little ideas that could make a big impact towards your long-term rest.

Entertainment and vacations have their place. They're fun and can be enjoyable. But their emphasis on activity reinforces the busyness of modern life rather than offering you the deeper renewal that your soul craves— the renewal that God made you to enter into and enjoy.

In that sense, reclaiming a regular rhythm of rest is truly countercultural. Would you consider trying a few of these?

MAIN POINT

The weekly Sabbath provides the pattern for regular daily rest and for less regular retreat-rests.

QUESTIONS FOR REFLECTION

- Are there smaller patterns of daily rest that are already built into your life?
- What could you consider doing more regularly to pull back from the busyness of your daily schedule that might help you feel more restored?
- Have you been on a youth retreat before? What were some of the rest-related benefits that you experienced from that?

9. So, if Rest is this Wonderful ... Why is it so Hard to Do?

Given all the benefits that come from the rest that God offers—and commands—wouldn't you expect His people to gladly take advantage of it?

Sadly, that's not the case. Instead, Scripture and our own experience show that we strongly resist resting. We act like this is an awful command.

Now, why is that? Why is something that's so good, so universally ignored by those who love the Lord and are loved by Him?

Here are a couple things you find in Scripture—see if any of them ring true for you ... I know all of them do for me.

Fear of not having enough. The very first people to hear of anything like a 1-in-7-day command to rest, refused it before they could even process the implications of what they were rejecting.

God had just brought the Israelites out of Egypt into the wilderness. And it's a place where they can't provide food for themselves— that's obvious. So, He tells them that He will give them manna, bread that appears on the ground each morning. They are to go out and gather it each day, except on the seventh, because that's a day to rest.

On the day before, the sixth, He will give them twice as much and He will keep it from spoiling an extra day, so that it will feed them on the seventh day as well (Exod. 16:4-5, 21-26).

He's telling them that He will take care of their physical needs. That they don't have to worry because He loves them.

But when the seventh day rolls around, a number of them go out looking for breakfast anyway (Exod. 16:27-30). They figure they have to work because, otherwise, they might not have what they need. They're scared that life might not turn out like they want it to, and so they don't rest.

Rejection of God's Authority. Fear often drives our busyness, but so does our basic human attitude toward God that says, 'Don't tell me how to live! I can make my own decisions.' While some of you may never say it that explicitly, it's a common message we find in our culture. Statements like, 'Follow your heart.' or 'You do you' capture the pride that naturally hides in all of our hearts, because of sin.

You see that attitude expressed by the man in Numbers 15:32-36 who went out to gather firewood on the Sabbath day.

This is well after God gave His Ten Commandments to the Israelites, telling them how to live with Him (Exod. 20:1-17) and long after he'd proven His love and care to them. The man had no excuse on that front.

And he doesn't seem to have wanted one. He claims no extenuating circumstances surrounding his disobedience and he goes out in broad daylight where everyone can see what he's doing. What stands out is his blatant contempt for God's command to rest.

The only way to account for his actions is to realize that when given a choice between what he wanted to do and what God told him was best, he chose the same path that our first parents, Adam and Eve, did. He honored his own ideas as superior to God's. And he didn't rest.

Feel burdened by life's responsibilities. For others of us, it's neither fear nor rebellion that keeps us jacked up, as much as we don't see how life could be any different. A woman named Martha falls into this category.

Jesus and His disciples dropped by to visit her home. Martha's sister, Mary, saw this as an opportunity to sit with Jesus and absorb His care. Martha sees none of that (Luke 10:38-42).

Or maybe it's better to say that she sees something else more. She sees the pressure of her societal obligations to show hospitality, and that drives everything else out of her mind.

Jesus, while not denying any of the work of being hospitable, tells Martha that she needs to see better than she does. He says that Mary has chosen something better and that it won't be taken from her.

Mary had eyes to see past the crushing weight of responsibilities that drives so much of our busyness. Many of us don't, which keeps us from stopping and choosing something better—from choosing to rest with the Lord.

Longing to have more than we do. For others of us, however, it's a matter of simple greed—of being discontent with what we can get from the other six days.

You hear that in passages where God calls people out who look like they're obeying Him by not working, but whose hearts are not really in it. Instead, they yearn for the Sabbath just to be over so that they can get back to making money (Amos 8:5).

Or worse, He calls out hypocrites. The Day of Atonement was the only day when God commanded the Israelites to fast, designating it explicitly as a day of Sabbath rest (Lev. 23:26-32). But later, He indicts His people for going through the motions of fasting, while exploiting those who worked for them (Isa. 58:3). They went through the motions of resting themselves, while driving others to work.

Or consider the Sabbath year. God extended the principle of the weekly Sabbath to the land so that every seventh year, it was to rest. The people were not to farm that year, but solely trust the Lord to provide for them (Lev. 25:1-7). That was a command the Israelites refused to obey (2 Chron. 36:21, Jer. 25:11-12). Their refusal, combined with their unwillingness to delight in a weekly rest, factored into why God sent them into exile (Lev. 26:34-35, Neh. 13:18, Jer. 17:27).

Yet, even when they returned from exile, they were still drawn away from resting by the allure of what they could get by engaging in commercial activities on the seventh day (Neh. 13:15).

Our unwillingness to be content with what God gives us is a chief theme throughout Scripture. It's a significant reason we refuse to rest.

And so, for many of us, this special 1-in-7 holy day becomes a day like any other. A day to catch up on the things that we didn't get to earlier in the week.

When that happens, Sabbath and resting may sound like nice ideas, but ones that are a little naïve. Certainly not things that fit into the modern world. They may be nice ideals. Things that really well-off people can afford. But things that are at best, inconvenient, or that will set you even further back than you already are.

And so, lots of people feel free to ignore resting. We ignore it without wondering if there's a connection between our spiritual state and our refusal to rest.

At the bare minimum, God says, 'Here's a day of delight. A day of rest. A day to recharge your spiritual batteries. A day that I have blessed and made holy.'

And we're like, 'Yeah, … no. You don't understand. I've got things I have to do.'

And then we get up Monday morning wondering why we feel spiritually flat. Stale. Why we don't feel rested, ready to go. Why we're not overflowing inside.

Sabbath may not be the whole answer to why you feel like that. But if you're not feeling spiritually energized Monday morning and you're blowing off the fourth commandment … maybe it's worth re-thinking.

Or maybe it's worth considering one other dimension to resting in the next chapter that we haven't yet touched on.

MAIN POINT

Our hearts generate lots of reasons that justify ignoring God's command to rest.

QUESTIONS FOR REFLECTION

- Do you sometimes think of Sunday as a day to catch up on things that you weren't able to get to earlier in the week?

- Can you identify with any of the above reasons for not resting—fear of not having enough, rebellion against God, burdened by your own or other people's expectations, or greed?

- Are there other reasons that make obeying God's command to rest seem impossible? How does His Word help you think about those?

10. We Rest Because We've Been Rescued

Moses records the Sabbath command in two different places, each of which offers a different reason for keeping it holy.

We saw in Exodus 20:8-11 that God anchors the day in Creation. When you come to Deuteronomy 5:12-15, however, you learn that he also grounds it in Salvation—in his work of delivering Israel from Egyptian slavery.

The command to rest is still the same, but now you see an additional dimension to it. Whereas Exodus acknowledges God-the-Creator, Deuteronomy highlights God-the-Redeemer, God-the-Rescuer.

His people had no choice in Egypt. They were forced into a life of hard labor. No rests. No relief. Just inescapable servitude—a life of endless, uninterrupted days of toil, dominated by enemies who hated them.

Then God freed them. And instead of demanding, like their former king, that they work without ceasing, He required the opposite. He insisted that they stop once a week to rest and based it on what He had done for them—that because he rescues the driven-ones they, as the rescued, can now rest.

And the key word in this (very good!) command is: remember—

*You shall **remember** that you were a slave in the land of Egypt, and the LORD your God brought you out from there with a mighty hand and an outstretched arm. Therefore the LORD your God commanded you to keep the Sabbath day. (Deut. 5:15, emphasis added).*

So, what are you supposed to remember? First, that you were a slave in Egypt. Now, don't say, 'Well, that doesn't apply to me—I've never even been to Egypt,' because neither had most of the people who first heard this.

The book of Deuteronomy is essentially a (very long) sermon that Moses gave shortly before his death. That means nearly all the people who had personally lived in Egypt, had died off by this time. And so, Moses was talking to their children and to their grandchildren.

So, why does he say, 'Remember that you were a slave in Egypt'? It's because this story of the Israelites in Egypt becomes the model for how you understand who you are and how God engages you.

This is how Scripture works. God often helps you understand the spiritual world, which you can't see, by first pointing to something in the physical world that you can.

For example, Scripture repeatedly returns to this theme of being a slave in Egypt to help you understand the nature of your own spirituality. It shows you that because sin entered the world, that you are born with a bentness that you can't change. A bentness that rules you and keeps you from wanting to be like God.

Now, that's not how you were made to be. The story of Creation teaches you that you are an image of God—that you are like Him and that you are made to like what He likes and to live a life like He lives. The Creation account sets the trajectory for understanding how much worth and value and dignity you have as a human being.

But after sin enters the picture, there's another trajectory that moves you away from the glory that God intended for you. Now, you're a broken image—not like Him in a fundamental way because you're born into sin—into spiritual slavery.

And Scripture teaches that you can't fix yourself. That sin owns you. That it forces you to do things because it compels you; gives you no other option.

It's that sense of addiction—of being enslaved by work, sex, alcohol, approval, respect, appearance, shopping, studies, whatever. It's that feeling of having no choice, like you can't say 'no', so that it's the only thing you can think about and that there's no way to be free from it.

And God tells you that a very important spiritual exercise is to take time, on a regular basis, to remember how that's been true of you—to remember that you were a slave in the land of Egypt.

But he says, 'Remember more than that. Because that's no longer true.' You were a slave in Egypt, but the Lord your God brought you out from there. You couldn't rescue yourself from sin's hold on you, but he could. And he did.

And so, you need to remember a number of things. You remember:

- that He keeps His promises to rescue you;
- that He's more powerful than all of your enemies combined;
- that He cares about you like no one else ever has;
- and that He loves you and has amazing plans for you and for this world that He wants to bring you into.

You remember what He's done, and you remember what that makes you now—a child of God, not a slave to sin. You remember that you're now family—part of His family—and that you can never lose your place in His family, because you can never lose your place in His heart.

And you remind yourself that this is all totally dependent on His kindness to you and not on anything that you've done. You remember that it really is by grace that you have been saved— not by reading the right books, listening to the right people, being in the right circles or by doing the right things—that it is by grace through faith in Jesus Christ that you have been saved. And that this is purely the grace-gift of God (Eph. 2:8-9).

You spend time remembering, so that what is true of you and of God, moves from the back of your mind to the front.

So, that's *what* we need to remember, but why is this important enough to carve out time in your busy schedule for it?

It's because the Hebrew word for 'remember' involves more than simple cognition. It's not like studying for a history test on ancient Israel. I'm sure you've had a test you crammed for, but once the test was over you completely forgot all the information you stayed up late memorizing. This is different. You're not trying to remember facts and figures, people and places, dates and times so that you can regurgitate them.

Instead, remembering means that you recall the past in such a way that it affects you in the present.

You spend time remembering so that the themes of Scripture inform and change how you think about life, how you feel about yourself, how you act toward others and how you interact with God.

You meditate on how helpless it feels to be trapped in sin—especially when you can't stop yourself—until you become aware again of how little you can do to help yourself.

And you recall God's kindness to step in and rescue you from your helplessness. And you keep remembering until you feel thankful again for all that He's done for you. Until what He's done and who He is kindles—rekindles—your passion for Him.

See, if we don't spend time remembering, we end up thinking too highly of ourselves and our own goodness, while thinking too little of God and His goodness. The net result is that we take Him for granted. And we lose passion for Him.

How do you regain that passion? You set aside time to think—to recall that you've never been a match for the evil inside of you that enslaves you.

And you remember that God's fundamental attitude toward you, in light of your inability, is to care about how helpless you are. To care so much that he rescued you from yourself when you couldn't. And as you consider how He's loved you in the past, you realize that He still does, right now.[1]

---

1. It's impossible to overstate how important this kind of remembering is because it's the primary way that we grow in our faith. In that respect, it's a key engine of our spiritual growth.

MAIN POINT

Remember what God has done for you in the past and that tells you how He thinks and feels about you now.

QUESTIONS FOR REFLECTION

- How often do you spend time remembering what God has done for you to save you from the penalty and power of sin?
- When you think about Jesus dying for you, do you trace what He did back to His heart behind why He did it—to His love and compassion for you?
- How hard is it to remind yourself that the same love that moved Jesus to rescue you, is the same love and attitude that he has for you now?

11. Learning to Live within Divinely Set Boundaries

I don't know if you think like this, but 'boundaries' can often sound negative. It seems like many people think this way. Boundaries sound like something that limits our fun or keeps us from being totally free. Scripture, however, gives us a totally different perspective.

Everything in Creation has built-in limits placed on it by the Creator. Neither night nor day reign supreme over the other, but each come at the times God sets for them (Jer. 33:20, Gen. 1:14, Ps. 104:19). The seasons of summer and winter follow each other—neither replacing the other—because God sets their boundaries as He does those of all the earth (Ps. 74:17, Eccl. 3:1). Or think about the sea with its proud, violent waves ... whose reach is set—limited—by the Lord (Jer. 5:22).

God alone is completely unbounded. He's the only one who can do whatever He likes, as He likes, when He likes. He's the only one who never encounters an internal limitation or an imposed constraint that affects what He can and cannot do.

Human beings, however, as part of His creation and by his good design, are inherently limited. We have to eat and drink on a regular basis, sleep a certain amount and exercise. We have certain God-created boundaries that limit what we can and cannot do.

Yes, we can push past those limits, but if you ignore them too strongly or too often, you will pay. You'll get weak, tired, fuzzy in your thinking or your body will turn on itself and start to physically break down. Each one of us has a different range to our limitations— different settings if you will—but none of us are unlimited.

And those limitations extend to our personalities and abilities. You have certain tolerances for how much social interaction you need and can handle—some people need more and some need less. But both are limitations.

You have different levels of interest in the various things you find in the universe. Your taste for the many different activities or areas of study that are possible, is unequal. Some you like a lot. Others you don't really care for. Yes, you can stretch that interest, but only to a certain amount. Why? Because you're limited.

Those aspects of your personality make you unique in the kingdom of God. As do your gifts and talents. That makes you indispensable in the body of Christ, so that God's people need you. But it's equally true that there are many, many more abilities that you don't have that others do.

And that's where you see the beauty of the limits that God builds into each of us. Because not only do God's people need you, but you also need them. He's made you and the rest of the Church to be interdependent so that we're better together as we reflect what He's like. We're stronger and more beautiful together than we could ever be on our own.

In other words, God likes you with the limitations you have—He celebrates them— and says that what He makes and the way He designs it is good and very good. And that includes the way He made you. Your limitations do not offend Him.

Instead, it's offensive when you reject them—when you think that you would be a better you, a more God-glorifying you, without them. It's offensive when you consistently push past the limits He gave you because of your own or other people's expectations of you.

And that's when God invites you to remember that:

In returning [in repentance] and rest you shall be saved; in quietness and in trust shall be your strength (Isa. 30:15).

Constant activity won't give you life. But inner renewal comes from quiet resting—trusting—in the Lord and in how He organizes the world.

Refuse God's invitation to realign with Him, however, and anything you run to, instead of Him, will only leave you that much more frantic and worn out. That's what God's people found out as Isaiah continued prophesying what life is like when you reject God's invitation to return and rest.

But you were unwilling, and you said:

'No! We will flee upon horses'; therefore you shall flee away; and, "We will ride upon swift steeds'; therefore your pursuers shall be swift.

A thousand shall flee at the threat of one; at the threat of five you shall flee, till you are left like a flagstaff on the top of a mountain, like a signal on a hill (Isa. 30:16-17).

What is 'fleeing'? It's a refusal to live in the world that is. A refusal to live in the world that God has made. And it's what you do when you think you know how best to handle life—when you believe that you know what you most need in life. It's a refusal to live within what God thinks is best.

Sadly, the result of chasing after what you think will save you—what will give you a good life apart from God—is that you'll never stop running.

Take God up on His offer to repent and rest, however, and you'll discover that the Lord longs to be gracious to you, even when you've tried to live in ways that ignore how He's made you (Isa. 30:18).

So, how do you know when you've been living past your limits and need to repent? Here are some red flags that tell you that you might be:

- Pay attention to when you feel anxious about all the things you're trying to do because it seems like there's no way to get them all done.

- Or notice when you seem to be in constant motion, never having time to rest or reflect on your life, but instead filling it endlessly with music, videos and social media.
- Or watch when you consistently cut out restorative things like sleep or time with family and friends because you have so many other things to do.
- Or pay attention to when you short-change your relationship with God by missing time in Scripture or prayer to fit something else in.
- Or take seriously when you're upset by God's commands to rest. Notice when they feel burdensome or when you try to argue with them in your own mind.

Those are all indicators that you're trying—maybe trying again—to live a life without limits. They're indications that it's time to repent and to rest again in Him, accepting the limitations that He's given you. Accepting them gladly, because you know that He's a loving Father who only ever wants what is best for you.

MAIN POINT

God invites us to live within the limits that He has set for us and our lives.

QUESTIONS FOR REFLECTION

- Do you believe that God likes you the way He made you—including your gifts, talents, personality traits and the limitations that come with each of them?
- Do you tend to push past your physical and emotional limits or have you learned to live within the boundaries that God's given you?
- How hard is it for you to just sit and be still … or is it easier to fill all the spaces of your life with scrolling or streaming?

12. Conclusion: Reordering Your World so that it Works

Well, we're nearly at the end of this little book, but, you may have noticed that I left some things hanging from the last chapter. I ended by giving us ways to realize when we've pushed past our limits, but that's kind of negative. So, let me wrap up by considering what it looks like to live inside your limitations—what it means to repent when you figure out that you've ignored the boundaries that God gave you.

First, start by talking to the Lord. Ask Him to forgive you for making human expectations more important than His. This is how you start turning your back on a rebellious approach to life.

But then, second, start moving in a more godly direction by thanking Him for making you limited in the ways that you are.

Thank Him that you need to eat and need to rest. Thank Him that you can't just keep going, saying, 'yes' to every opportunity that comes your way. Ask Him to help you celebrate how He's made you by agreeing with Him that His designs for you are very good.

And then third, you have to make some practical decisions about how to live within your limitations. If you feel anxious and overwhelmed, and won't take time to rest, then accept the obvious conclusion: you're trying to do things that God hasn't given you to do. You're living like Jesus wouldn't.

I'm always amazed to hear Him pray to the Father the night before He's arrested and say, 'I glorified you on earth, having accomplished the work that you gave me to do' (John 17:4).

Think about what that means. Jesus went to the cross with absolutely nothing left on His 'to-do' list. Nothing left undone because He accomplished—finished—what God gave Him to do.

In a very real sense, that means he went to bed every night (as he accepted another part of his human limitations!) having done all the things that God gave Him to do for that day— that He didn't do less than God gave Him and He didn't try to do more.

And what amazes me even more is that He could say He did everything even though there was still so much to do. There had to be lepers in the area who hadn't yet been cleansed, blind people who still couldn't see, paralytics who couldn't move as they should and others who were tormented by evil spirits (i.e., Acts 3:1-10, 5:12-16).

And you would think—I would think—that surely there was one more thing He wanted to teach the disciples before they took over leading the church. At least one more parable, right?

Wrong. Jesus said He did everything the Father gave Him to do. That's what allowed Him to say 'no' to people at different times (i.e., Matt. 12:38-39, 16:1-4; Luke 10:38-42, 12:13-14; John 6:15, 6:26ff, 7:3, 11:3(21), 18:19-21, 18:33-34).

Jesus knew what He had to say 'yes' to. He knew what the Father expected from Him— the things that if He didn't do, then He'd sin against God. And it was in knowing what He had to do, that then gave Him the freedom not to do everything that everyone around Him wanted from Him.

You and I need the same knowledge. There will always be more things that you could do—

more good things—than you can get to in any one lifetime. That means you'll have to say 'no' to many things over the course of your life in order to live well within how God has made you. Knowing what you have to say 'yes' to, helps you say 'no' to everything else with a clear conscience.

So, how do you learn what those 'yes' things are? There's no quick answer to that.

Some things in Scripture are clear—like loving your parents—if you don't love them, then no one else will in the unique way that you can and that God expects from you. That's part of what He's given you to accomplish that's even different from any siblings you might have.

Even there though, you still have to think clearly about God's expectations because sometimes parents can want things from their children that are wrong to want—things they expect from you that God doesn't.

Other decisions are less clear—should you take harder classes at school or easier ones, play a sport or an instrument or neither, date someone or not just yet, join a summer missions team or get a part-time job, go to college or go to work? How do you learn what God expects from you when there's no one right answer that fits every person, at all times, in all places?

Part of the answer is to rely on the resources God's given you. Obviously, you think through Scripture to see if there are wise principles that apply. But you also lean on His people by asking for good biblical counsel from your family, your youth pastors and from godly friends.

You can also learn a lot by reflecting on some of your past experiences. As I meditate on choices I've made, there are a number of them that I would make again. It's clear, as I think about the good things that came out of them for me or for other people, that that was something the Lord had given me to do.

Hindsight, however, makes equally clear the many mistakes I've made. I can see looking back, that there are things I've chosen to do for the wrong reasons. Or things that I've chosen to do that were good, but that kept me from doing something even better. Or things that I realized later just aren't suited for who God has made me.

I've grown a lot in my understanding of what God has given me to do by reflecting on the past things that I've done. Learning what

He expects from you is not quite trial-and-error, but it does take time.

It also takes a willingness to consider that sometimes you've said 'yes' to things, when you should have said, 'no'. What lets you consider that? One last time, it's Jesus' work that lets you now rest.

Part of what He accomplished was to pay for the many times when you haven't done what God's given you—for the times when you rejected the goodness of God's balanced world, to create one for yourself of anxiety, driven activity and frantic entertainment.

Jesus paid for each one of those decisions, so that what? So that you could enter back into a world where you're right with God, willing to live within the boundaries of what God's given you. Retake your place now in His larger world and as he promised, you will find rest for your soul (Matt. 11:29).

And now, may your soul find rest in God,
May he be your rock and your salvation,
the one who provides for you,
so that you will never be shaken.
(Based on Ps. 62:1-2)

Appendix A: What Now?

═══════

All of us struggle in some way in our relationship with work and rest. Do you have a sense of which side you tend to fall off on of over-working or over-resting?

Make a list of all the ways you work now (i.e. the ways you are productive and creative in this world, either in school, at home, with a job, in outside hobbies and activities, etc.).

Have you ever tried practicing a Sabbath—of resting from your work in any way? If not, what are the top reasons that keep you from doing so?

Make a list of the people who influence how much you work and rest (i.e. parents, friends, God's, yourself, etc.). Rank those voices from most influential to least.

Take ten minutes and meditate on:

- what you need Jesus to forgive and free you from as you deal with the areas of work and rest,
- what Jesus did to forgive and free you,
- how much He loved you to do that,
- how He still feels that same way about you … and then spend some time talking to Him about what you're thinking and feeling.

There's always a next step for each of us as we mature in our faith, so think about what that might be for you in the areas of work and rest.

Have you tried taking a Sabbath before?

What would it look like to extend some kind of rest from over-work and busyness into another part of your week?

Could you consider taking fifteen minutes to sit quietly with no distractions and allow yourself the headspace just to think or pray?

Appendix B: Further Reading

On assessing and understanding the dangers of our modern rest-less world:

DeYoung, Kevin. *Crazy Busy: A (Mercifully) Short Book about a (Really) Big Problem*, Crossway 2013.

On the Sabbath (theological underpinnings):

Ryken, Philip. 'The Fourth Commandment: Work and Leisure' chapter in *Written in Stone: The Ten Commandments and Today's Moral Crisis*, Crossway Books, 2013.

Westminster Confession of Faith XX.7-8, *Larger Catechism Questions* 115-121, *Shorter Catechism Questions* 57-62.

On the interplay of Work and Rest:

Comer, John Mark. *Garden City: Work, Rest, and the Art of Being Human*, Zondervan, 2015.

Sayers, Dorothy. 'Why Work?' chapter in *Letters to a Diminished Church*, Thomas Nelson Inc, 2004

Christian Focus Publications

Our mission statement —

STAYING FAITHFUL

In dependence upon God we seek to impact the world through literature faithful to His infallible Word, the Bible. Our aim is to ensure that the Lord Jesus Christ is presented as the only hope to obtain forgiveness of sin, live a useful life and look forward to heaven with Him.

Our books are published in four imprints:

CHRISTIAN
FOCUS

Popular works including biographies, commentaries, basic doctrine and Christian living.

CHRISTIAN
HERITAGE

Books representing some of the best material from the rich heritage of the church.

MENTOR

Books written at a level suitable for Bible College and seminary students, pastors, and other serious readers. The imprint includes commentaries, doctrinal studies, examination of current issues and church history.

CF4•K

Children's books for quality Bible teaching and for all age groups: Sunday school curriculum, puzzle and activity books; personal and family devotional titles, biographies and inspirational stories — because you are never too young to know Jesus!

Christian Focus Publications Ltd,
Geanies House, Fearn, Ross-shire,
IV20 1TW, Scotland, United Kingdom.
www.christianfocus.com
blog.christianfocus.com